WHERE IN THE WORLD IS KOREA?

KOREAN PENINSULA

is located in Asia, bordered by China to the northwest, Russia to the northeast, and neighbors Japan to the east across the East Sea.

Since 1948, it has been divided between two distinct sovereign states: North Korea and South Korea.

LOCATION

Seoul, South Korea
Latitude 37° 33' 57.60" N
Longitude 126° 58' 42.24" E

Pyeongyang, North Korea
Latitude 39° 02' 1.86" N
Longitude 125° 45' 15.55" E

RUSSIA
EUROPE ASIA
CHINA
NORTH
AMERICA
JAPAN
MIDDLE
EAST
AFRICA
SOUTH
AMERICA
AUSTRALIA

 ADDITIONAL FACTS

**219,155 KM²
(84,616 SQ MI)**

**WATER
2.8%**

**77 MIL (2017 EST.)
SOUTH 52 MIL
NORTH 25 MIL**

CHINA

NORTH
KOREA

• PYEONGYANG

EAST SEA

• SEOUL

DOK-DO

SOUTH
KOREA

YELLOW SEA

JAPAN

JEJU-DO

HOW FAR IS KOREA?

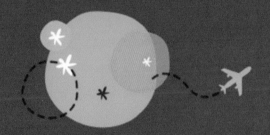

FLIGHT DURATION / HOURS / DISTANCE TO SEOUL (KM)

	City	Duration	Distance
🇨🇳	Beijing	2:00	592km / 952mi
🇯🇵	Tokyo	2:40	716km / 1,152mi
🇵🇭	Manila	4:00	1,628km / 2,620mi
🇻🇳	Ho Chi Minh	5:00	2,237km / 3,599mi
🇷🇺	Moscow	8:40	4,103km / 6,601mi
🇦🇪	Abu Dhabi	8:40	4,288km / 6,899mi
🇩🇪	Frankfurt	10:25	5,310km / 8,544mi
🇦🇺	Sydney	10:45	5,173km / 8,324mi
🇬🇧	London	11:00	5,502km / 8,852mi
🇫🇷	Paris	11:00	5,569km / 8,960mi
🇪🇬	Cairo	13:20*	5,270km / 8,480mi
🇺🇸	New York	14:00	6,865/ 11,046mi
🇰🇪	Nairobi	16:00*	6,279km / 10,103mi
🇧🇷	Sao Paulo	25:45*	11,392km / 18,330mi
🇨🇱	Santiago	27:30*	11,401km / 18,345mi

*AS OF 2018, THERE ARE NO DIRECT FLIGHTS BETWEEN THE TWO PLACES

HOW BIG IS KOREA?

VISUAL COMPARISON

United States (9,833,000 km²) is 45 times as big as Korean peninsula (220,847 km²).

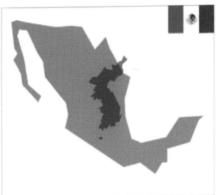

Mexico (1,964,375 km²) is 8.9 times as big as Korean peninsula (220,847 km²).

France (551,695 km²) is 2.5 times as big as Korean peninsula (220,847 km²).

Germany (357,114 km²) is 1.62 times as big as Korean peninsula (220,847 km²).

United Kingdom (242,900 km²) is 1.1 times as big as Korean peninsula (220,847 km²).

Korean peninsula (220,847 km²) is 1.25 times as big as Uruguay (176,215 km²).

Korean peninsula (220,847 km²) is 1.12 times as big as Senegal (196,722 km²).

Korean peninsula (220,847 km²) is 2.1 times as big as Iceland (103,000 km²).

Korean peninsula (220,847 km²) is 5.1 times as big as Denmark (43,094 km²).

HOW MUCH
IS THE
KOREAN WON?

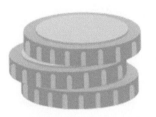

As of December 2018

1 USD = 1,128 KRW

1 CAD = 843 KRW

1 RMB = 163 KRW

1 HKD = 144 KRW

1 JPY = 9.94 KRW

1 GBP = 1,409 KRW

1 MXN = 55 KRW

1 EUR = 1,276 KRW

WHAT TIME IS IT IN KOREA?

WHEN IT'S **JAN 01, 2019 01:00 AM** IN **Seoul**

DEC 31, 2018
08:00 AM
las vegas

DEC 31, 2018
10:00 AM
mexico city

DEC 31, 2018
02:00 PM
rio de janeiro

DEC 31, 2018
04:00 PM
london

DEC 31, 2018
05:00 PM
paris

DEC 31, 2018
07:00 PM
moscow

DEC 31, 2018
07:00 PM
nairobi

DEC 31, 2018
07:30 PM
tehran

DEC 31, 2018
09:30 PM
new delhi

JAN 1, 2019
00:00 AM
shanghai

JAN 1, 2019
01:00 AM
tokyo

JAN 1, 2019
03:00 AM
sidney

THE SOUTH KOREAN FLAG

WHAT DO ALL THE SYMBOLS MEAN?

태극기 太極旗
[TAE-GEUK-GI]

literal meaning
"Supreme Ultimate Flag"

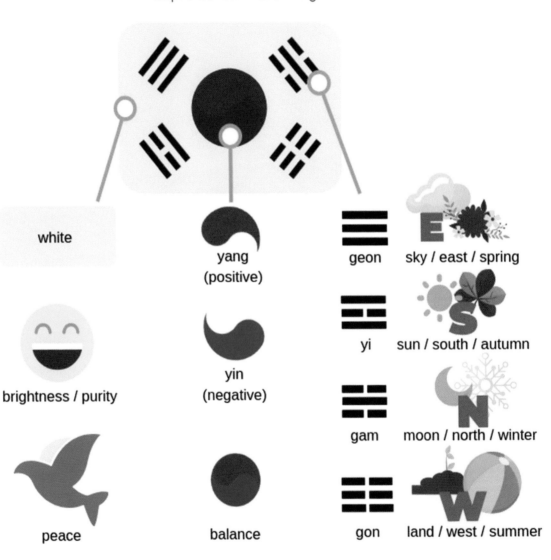

white

brightness / purity

peace

yang
(positive)

yin
(negative)

balance

geon — sky / east / spring

yi — sun / south / autumn

gam — moon / north / winter

gon — land / west / summer

the national characteristic of loving brightness, purity, and peace

the rules of the mother nature where the whole creation revolves around the interaction between yin and yang

the 4 symbols form harmony of unity, centered around the yin and yang symbol

THE NORTHKOREAN FLAG

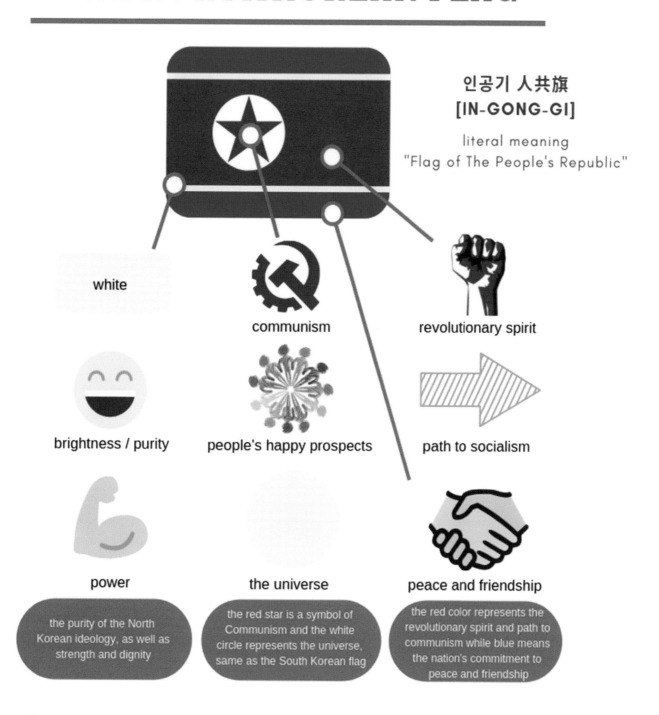

인공기 人共旗
[IN-GONG-GI]

literal meaning
"Flag of The People's Republic"

white

communism

revolutionary spirit

brightness / purity

people's happy prospects

path to socialism

power

the universe

peace and friendship

the purity of the North Korean ideology, as well as strength and dignity

the red star is a symbol of Communism and the white circle represents the universe, same as the South Korean flag

the red color represents the revolutionary spirit and path to communism while blue means the nation's commitment to peace and friendship

History of In Gong Gi

When WWI ended with an Allied victory in 1945 , Japan relinquished its control over Korea and the Soviet Union occupied the northern half of Korea while the US occupying the southern half, per Allied terms. Since then, the Soviet Union leaders thought that inheriting the traditional Taegukgi was inappropriate, and decided to design a new flag. Kim Il-Sung, the then leader of North Korea yielded, and 1947, a new flag was dictated from Moscow.

HISTORY OF TAE GEUK GI

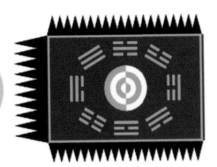

The King's Flag

Flag of the King Jeongjo 정조 (ca. 1800) of The Joseon Dynasty (1392-1897). The named Eo-gi 어기 and is in the Kyujanggak 규장각, Seoul National Univ.

1800

1882

The Debut

Park Yeong-hyo creates the very first Taeguki, which was a modified version of the King's Flag. Now it represents more than just the king - a nation

The Flag of The Empire

The Great Korean Empire 대한제국 [dae-han-je-guk] 大韓帝國 was proclaimed in October 1897 by Emperor Gojong of the Joseon Dynasty

1897 | 1910

1919 | 1948

Symbol of Resistance

During the Japanese occupation, a flag similar to the current South Korean flag was used by the provisional Korean government based in China

Symbol of Prosperity

Following the establishment of the South Korean state in 1948, the current flag was declared official on October 15, 1949,

today

OFFICIAL NATIONAL SYMBOLS
OF KOREA

1. Guk Sae 국새 - It's an official seal for state affairs and an important national symbol. It is used on important state documents, as it represents national authority, the nation's power and culture. The current, fifth, guk sae is made of a combination of gold, silver, copper, zinc, and iridium, and is square in shape and measures 10.4 centimeters on all sides, with a weight of 3.38 kilograms. It's engraved with the letters dae han min guk 대한민국 ("Great Republic of Korea"), with a pair of phoenix seating.

2. Guk Jang 국장 – It's the national emblem of Korea, and is based on the motifs of other national symbols - the Korean flag and the mu gung hwa flower. It's used as a state symbol on major documents sent to foreign institutions, on medals and other decorations, as well as Presidential commendations, and signage on diplomatic missions abroad.

3. The emblem of the National Government is a stylized Taeguk ("supreme ultimate"), an essential part of the Asian philosophy.

4. Tae Kwon Do - The Way of The Hand and Foot - Tae Kwon Do has been a way for the Korean people to train not just their bodies but their minds through difficult times. Today, it's a globally recognized sport with more than 80 million people practicing. It officially became Korea's national sport in 2018.

5. Mu Gung Hwa 무궁화 – The rose of Sharon, which literally means "eternal blossom that never fades" in Korean, is a symbol of the indomitable Korean spirit, just like how the flower can persevere through harsh weather conditions and eventually blossom in the end. The flower has been loved by the Koreans from the ancient Korean kingdom of Gojoseon. The ancient Chinese literature referred to Korea as the "land of wise men where mu gung hwa blooms."

6. Seal of the President, with two phoenixes facing each other over a rose of Sharon.

7. Emblem of the National Assembly. The word "국회" meaning 'National Assembly' appears in Hangul in the center of a rose of Sharon.

PROFILE

WHO LIVES IN SOUTH KOREA?

TOTAL POPULATION 51.25 mil. (2016)
MEDIAN AGE
TOTAL 41.8 years
MALE 40.2 years
FEMALE 43.4 years (2017 est.)
LIFE EXPECTANCY 81.3 (2010-2015)

NATIONALITIES OF FOREIGN NATIONALS

57.5%	China	8.5%	Vietnam
7.9%	USA	5.7%	Thailand
3.2%	Philippines	3.1%	Uzbekistan
2.9%	Japan	2.8%	Indonesia
2.6%	Cambodia	2%	Mongolia
2%	Nepal	1.9%	Chinese Taipei

POPULATION BY REGION

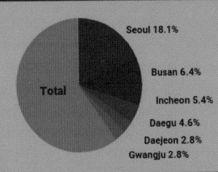

Seoul 18.1%
Busan 6.4%
Incheon 5.4%
Daegu 4.6%
Daejeon 2.8%
Gwangju 2.8%
Total

POPULATION DENSITY

BLOOD TYPE

A 34%
B 27%
O 27%
AB 12%

RELIGION

NON-RELIGIOUS
46.5%

BUDDHISM
22.8%

PROTESTANTISM
18.3%

CATHOLICISM
10.9%

AGE STRUCTURE

0-14 yrs	15-24 yrs	25-54 yrs	55-64 yrs	65+ yrs
13.21%	12.66%	45.52%	14.49%	14.12%

GENDER RATIO

Female
100

Male
99.84

As of December 2016

POPULATION TREND
(IN MILLIONS, 1950-2015)

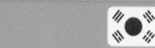

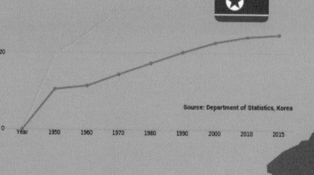

Source: Department of Statistics, Korea

| Year | 1950 | 1960 | 1970 | 1980 | 1990 | 2000 | 2010 | 2015 |

Chongjin (0.6 million)

Tanchon (0.3 million)

Hamhung (0.7 million)

Wonsan (1.5 million)

Pyongyang (3.2 million)

Nampo (0.3 million)

Seoul (9.9 million)

Incheon (2.8 million)

Daejeon (1.5 million)

Daegu (2.4 million)

Busan (3.4 million)

Gwangju (1.5 million)

ECONOMY

SOUTH KOREA

GDP RANK (NOMINAL) 11TH

US $1,655 TRILLION (2018)
GDP GROWTH 3.0% (2017)
GDP PER CAPITA US$ 32,774 (2018)

TRADING (2017)

EXPORTS **US $577.4 BILLION**

IMPORTS **US $457.5 BILLION**

MAIN EXPORT PARTNERS

CHINA	44%
USA	21.4%
VIETNAM	14.4%
HONG KONG	12.1%
JAPAN	8.2%

MAIN IMPORT PARTNERS

CHINA	44%
USA	21.4%
VIETNAM	14.4%
HONG KONG	12.1%
JAPAN	8.2%

LABOR FORCE

25 Million (2012 Est.)

UNEMPLOYMENT RATE

3.1% (Oct. 2015)

GDP BY SECTOR

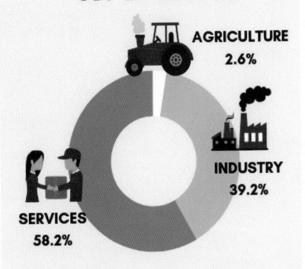

AGRICULTURE 2.6%

INDUSTRY 39.2%

SERVICES 58.2%

TOP 10 EXPORTS

1
Semiconductors: US$107.1 billion
(21.2% of total exports)

2
Oil Products: US$38.9 billion
(7.7% of total exports)

3
Cars: US$33.1 billion
(6.6% of total exports)

4
Flat Panel Displays & Sensors: US$20.7 billion
(4.1% of total exports)

5
Synthetic Resins: US$19.4 billion
(3.9% of total exports)

6
Car Parts: US$19.3 billion
(3.8% of total exports)

7
Steel Plates: US$16.7 billion
(3.3% of total exports)

8
Offshore Construction Structure and Parts:
US$15.9 billion (3.2% of total exports)

9
Wireless Communication Devices:
US$14.7 billion (2.9% of total exports)

10
Computers: US$9.2 billion
(1.8% of total exports)

NORTH KOREA

GDP RANK (NOMINAL) 125TH

US$ 28.5 BILLION (2016)
GDP GROWTH -3.5% (2017 EST.)
GDP PER CAPITA $1,300(2016)

TRADING (2016)

EXPORTS **US $2.985 BILLION**

IMPORTS **US $3.752 BILLION**

MAIN EXPORT PARTNERS

CHINA	87%
INDIA	2.5%
PHILIPPINES	1.9%
PAKISTAN	1%

MAIN IMPORT PARTNERS

CHINA	90%
INDIA	1.7%
THAILAND	1.5%
PHILIPPINES	1%

LABOR FORCE

14 Million (2014 Est.)

UNEMPLOYMENT RATE

25.6% (2013 Est.)

GDP BY SECTOR

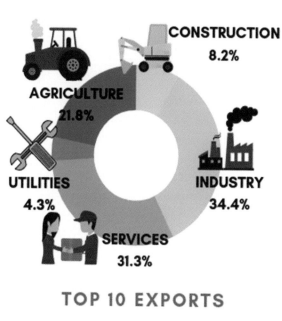

CONSTRUCTION 8.2%
AGRICULTURE 21.8%
INDUSTRY 34.4%
UTILITIES 4.3%
SERVICES 31.3%

TOP 10 EXPORTS

1. Clothing, accessories (not knit or crochet): US$499.8 million (27.1% of total exports)

2. Mineral fuels including oil: $420 million (22.8%)

3. Ores, slag, ash: $187.5 million (10.2%)

4. Fish: $164 million (8.9%)

5. Iron, steel: $83.2 million (4.5%)

6. Fruits, nuts: $79 million (4.3%)

7. Knit or crochet clothing, accessories: $65.7 million (3.6%)

8. Salt, sulphur, stone, cement: $44.2 million (2.4%)

9. Electrical machinery, equipment: $43.6 million (2.4%)

10. Machinery including computers: $35.2 million (1.9%)

AEGUKGA 애국가

NATIONAL ANTHEM OF KOREA

MEANING

愛國歌 Literally Meaning "Love Country Song" or "Patriotic Song"

COMPOSED BY

안익태 Ahn Eak-tai (1935)

BACKGROUND

Before the founding of South Korea, the song's lyrics, set to the music of "Auld Lang Syne", was sung, as well as during Korea under Japanese rule by dissidents. The version set to the melody composed by Ahn Eak-tai was adopted as the national anthem of the Korean exile government, which existed during Korea's occupation by Japan from the early 1910s to the mid-1940s. "Aegukga" has four verses, but on most occasions only the first one is performed at public events such as baseball games and soccer matches.

LYRICS EXPLAINED

Verse 1: 동해 물과 백두산이 마르고 닳도록 하느님이 보우하사 우리나라 만세.
Until that day when Mt. Baekdu is worn away and the East Sea's waters run dry, May God protect and preserve our country!
Refrain: 무궁화 삼천리 화려강산 대한 사람, 대한으로 길이 보전하세.
Hibiscus and three thousand ri full of splendid mountains and rivers; Great Koreans, to the Great Korean way, stay always true!

Verse 2: 남산 위에 저 소나무 철갑을 두른 듯 바람서리 불변함은 우리 기상일세.
As the pine atop Namsan Peak stands firm, unchanged through wind and frost, as if wrapped in armor, so shall our resilient spirit.
Refrain

Verse 3: 가을 하늘 공활한데 높고 구름 없이 밝은 달은 우리 가슴 일편단심일세.
The autumn skies are void and vast, high and cloudless; the bright moon is like our heart, undivided and true.
Refrain

Verse 4: 이 기상과 이 맘으로 충성을 다하여 괴로우나 즐거우나 나라 사랑하세.
With this spirit and this mind, let us give all loyalty, in suffering or joy, to love our nation.
Refrain

HOLIDAYS OF KOREA

2019

NEW YEAR'S DAY
(JAN 1)

Like many other countries, the first day of the Gregorian (Solar) calendar is celebrated, and many Korean visit the coast or the mountains to see the first sunrise of the year.

SEOLLAL
(FEB 4-6)

It's traditional Korean Lunar New Year's Day (Seollal), and is one of the most important holidays, much more significant than January 1st. Most people travel to their hometown to visit their family. On this day, Koreans put on Hanbok and bows to their elders, and eat tteokguk (rice cake soup) and mandu guk (dumpling soup). They also play traditional games like yutnori (traditional Korean board game), spinning tops, and flying kites.

INDEPENDENCE MOVEMENT DAY
(MAR 1)

This is the day of commemorating the Declaration of Independence, which was proclaimed on March 1, 1919, against the Japanese occupation.

CHILDREN'S DAY
(MAY 5)

This is the day all Korean kids wait for! Families celebrate with their kids, wishing them to grow up healthy and smart. They usually go out to amusement parks, zoos, or shopping malls (to buy gifts!)

BUDDHA'S BIRTHDAY
(MAY 12)

Korea traditionally has been a Buddhist country, and the traces are found everywhere, including this holiday. It's the eighth day of the fourth lunar month, and you can see beautifully decorated temples across the country.

MEMORIAL DAY
(JUNE 6)

It's a very emotional day for Koreans as it commemorates and honors the fallen soldiers and civilians who lost their lives fighting for their country during the Korean War. Ceremonies are held at the National Cemetery in Seoul

LIBERATION DAY
(AUG 15)

Korea became free from the Japanese occupation on this day, when they surrendered to the allies in 1945, ending the World War II.

CHUSEOK
(SEP 12-14)

Along with Seollal, it's another very important traditional holiday – on the 15th day of the 8th lunar month, Koreans celebrate for a successful harvest year and families get together for memorial rituals called charye, for their ancestors.

NATIONAL FOUNDATION DAY
(OCT 3)

According to the founding myth of Gojoseon, the first nation ever built on the Korean peninsula, the legendary god-king Dangun, proclaimed the beginning of the nation. The founding date, or 개천절 gae cheon jeol ("the heaven opening day") is celebrated at Cham Seong Dan Altar on top of Manisan Mt. in Ganghwado Island.

HANGEUL DAY
(OCT 9)

It's when the publication of Hun Min Jeong Eum ("The Proper Sounds for the Instruction of the People"), the basis of Korean Alphabet, Hangeul, was proclaimed in 1446, by King Sejong The Great.

CHRISTMAS
(DEC 25)

Korea has a large percentage of Christians, and Christmas is celebrated all over the country, where couples reaffirm their love and families get together for quality time.

COUNTRIES

THAT DON'T NEED A VISA TO VISIT KOREA

UP TO 180 DAYS

- CANADA

UP TO 90 DAYS

* Except Cyprus and Portugal
* For British passport holders, only British citizens and British National (Overseas) enjoy visa-free entry.
* Except for French passports issued in New Caledonia.

- EUROPEAN UNION CITIZENS*
- ANTIGUA AND BARBUDA
- AUSTRALIA
- BAHAMAS
- BARBADOS
- BRAZIL
- CHILE
- COLOMBIA
- COSTA RICA
- DOMINICA
- DOMINICAN REPUBLIC
- ECUADOR
- EL SALVADOR
- GRENADA
- GUATEMALA
- HAITI
- HONG KONG
- ICELAND
- ISRAEL
- JAMAICA
- JAPAN
- KUWAIT
- LIBERIA
- LIECHTENSTEIN
- MACAU
- MALAYSIA
- MEXICO
- MOROCCO
- NEW ZEALAND
- NICARAGUA
- NORWAY
- PANAMA
- PERU
- SAINT KITTS AND NEVIS
- SAINT LUCIA
- SAINT VINCENT AND THE GRENADINES
- SERBIA
- SINGAPORE
- SURINAME
- SWITZERLAND
- TAIWAN
- THAILAND
- TRINIDAD AND TOBAGO
- TURKEY
- UNITED ARAB EMIRATES
- UNITED STATES
- URUGUAY
- VENEZUELA

UP TO 60 DAYS

- LESOTHO
- PORTUGAL
- RUSSIA

UP TO 30 DAYS

** For French passports issued in New Caledonia

- ALBANIA
- ANDORA
- ARGENTINA
- BAHRAIN
- BOSNIA AND HERZEGOVINA
- BRUNEI
- CYPRUS
- ESWATINI
- FIJI
- GUYANA
- HONDURAS
- KAZAKHSTAN
- KIRIBATI
- MARSHALL ISLANDS
- MAURITIUS
- MICRONESIA
- MONACO
- MONTENEGRO
- NAURU
- NEW CALEDONIA**
- OMAN- PALAU
- PARAGUAY
- QATAR
- SAMOA
- SAN MARINO
- SAUDI ARABIA
- SEYSCHELLES
- SOLOMON ISLANDS
- SOUTH AFRICA
- TONGA
- TUNISIA
- TUVALU
- VATICAN CITY

As of April 2017 holders of normal passports of all countries require a visa to visit North Korea.

Holders of diplomatic or service passports issued to nationals of the following countries can visit North Korea without a visa.

- ALBANIA
- BELARUS
- BULGARIA
- CHINA
- CUBA
- INDONESIA
- IRAN
- KYRGYZSTAN
- LAOS
- MONGOLIA
- MONTENEGRO
- MYANMAR
- RUSSIA
- SERBIA
- SWITZERLAND
- SYRIA
- TAJIKISTAN
- UKRAINE
- VIETNAM
- ZIMBABWE

korean places

AND THEIR MEANINGS

SEOUL
서울
"Capital City"

PYONGYANG
평양 平壤
"Flat Land"

BUSAN
부산 釜山
"Cauldron Mountain"

DAEJEON
대전 大田
"Grand Field"

INCHEON
인천 仁川
"Kind River"

CHONGJIN
청진 清津
"Clear River Crossing"

HAMHUNG
함흥 咸興
"Total Prosperity"

DAEGU
대구 大邱
"Large Hill"

GWANGJU
광주 光州
"Province of Light"

WONSAN
원산 元山
"Circular Mountain"

TAE KWON DO

KOREAN MARTIAL ART AND NATIONAL SPORT

"The most difficult part of traditional Taekwondo is not learning the first kick or punch. It is not struggling to remember the motions of a poomsae or becoming acquainted with Korean culture. Rather, it is taking the first step across the threshold of the dojang door. This is where roads diverge, where choices are made that will resonate throughout a lifetime."

— DOUG COOK, TAEKWONDO: A PATH TO EXCELLENCE

WHAT THEY MEAN

태   권   도

TAE	KWON	DO
"TO STOMP" "FEET"	"FIST" "PUNCH"	"DISCIPLINE" "WAY"

"THE WAY OF THE HAND AND FOOT"

BY THE NUMBERS

MEMBER COUNTRIES	208
PEOPLE PRACTICING	OVER 80 MILLION
BLACK BELT HOLDERS	OVER 4 MILLION
TAE KWON DO STUDIOS IN KOREA	OVER 10,000

BRIEF HISTORY

1940'S 1950'S — **FIRST SCHOOLS ESTABLISHED**
Shortly after WWII, martial arts schools, named "KWAN"s appear, but each *kwan* practiced their own style of martial arts.

1952 — **EARLY FORMATION**
South Korean President Syngman Rhee urged that the martial arts styles of the kwans be merged.

1959 1966 — **KTA AND ITF ESTABLISHED**
Korea Taekwondo Association (KTA) was established to facilitate the unification of Korean martial arts.

In 1966, Choi established International Taekwondo Federation (ITF), a separate entity incorporating his own style.

1973 — **WORLD TAEKWONDO FEDRATION**
World Federation of Taekwondo Is Established, with Kukkiwon as headquarter.

2000 — **GLOBALLY RECOGNIZED**
Taekwondo became an official medal event at the 2000 games in Sydney

5 TENETS OF TAE KWON DO

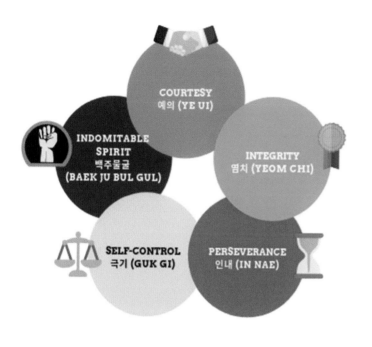

- COURTESY
  예의 (YE UI)
- INDOMITABLE SPIRIT
  백주물굴 (BAEK JU BUL GUL)
- INTEGRITY
  염치 (YEOM CHI)
- SELF-CONTROL
  극기 (GUK GI)
- PERSEVERANCE
  인내 (IN NAE)

TAE KWON DO OATH

1. I shall **observe** the **tenets** of Tae Kwon Do

2. I shall **respect** my **instructor** and **seniors**

3. I shall **never misuse** Tae Kwon Do

4. I shall be a **champion** of **freedom** & **justice**

5. I shall **build** a more **peaceful world**.

Tae Kwon Do has a ranking system, where ranks are typically divided by the levels prior to black (color belts, or 급 Kup), and the levels after black (품 Poom) as junior (below 15) and senior (단 Dan).

There are no official rules as to which color corresponds to which level, and for that reason, rank colors and order varies within schools and styles.

In traditional Tae Kwon Do system, there are only three color belts - White for all the Kup practitioners (10-1), Red for those eligible for the 1st Dan promotion exam, and Black for those above 1st Dan.

Today's Tae Kwon Do schools have adopted many different colors for different levels for Kup practitioners, in order to incentives their learning and provide motivation for continuing, especially the kids.

Some of the typical set up is illustrated on the side.

White	10 - 9 Kup
Yellow	8 Kup
Green	7 Kup
Blue	6 Kup
Purple	5 Kup
Orange	4 Kup
Brown	3 Kup
Red	2 - 1 Kup
Black	1 + Dan

사랑해요

Hangul 한글
The Korean Alphabet

KING SEJONG
THE GREAT
(1397 – 1450)

Inventor of Hangul

나랏말ᄊᆞ미 中듕國귁에 달아 文문字ᄍᆞ와로 서르ᄉᆞᄆᆞᆺ디 아니ᄒᆞᆯᄊᆡ 이런 젼ᄎᆞ로 어린 百ᄇᆡᆨ姓셩이 니르고져 ᄒᆞᇙ배이셔도 ᄆᆞᄎᆞᆷ내 제ᄠᅳ들 시러펴디 몯ᄒᆞᇙ노미 하니라 내 이ᄅᆞᆯ 爲윙ᄒᆞ야 어엿비너겨 새로 스믈여듧字ᄍᆞᄅᆞᆯ ᄆᆡᇰᄀᆞ노니 사ᄅᆞᆷ마다 ᄒᆡ여 수ᄫᅵ니겨 날로ᄡᅮ메 便뼌安ᅙᅡᆫᄒᆡ고져 ᄒᆞᇙᄯᆞᄅᆞ미니라

훈민정음
HUN MIN JEONG EUM

"The Proper Sounds
for the Instruction of the People"

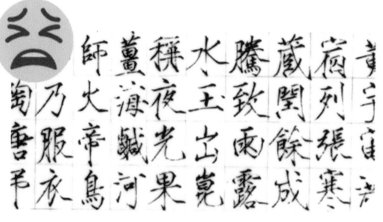

Before the creation of Hangul, Koreans primarily wrote using Classical Chinese, which prohibited lower class Koreans from learning it, thus making many illiterate. Also the difficulty of communication arising from vast differences between Korean and Chinese language was a factor in creating Hangul.

Seodang (Village School), ca 1780
Kim Hong Do

To promote literacy among the common people, King Sejong the Great, the fourth king of the Joseon Dynasty, created and promulgated a new alphabet.

The Korean alphabet was designed so that people with little education could learn to read and write. A popular saying about the alphabet is, "A wise man can acquaint himself with them before the morning is over; even a stupid man can learn them in the space of ten days."

The Korean alphabet faced opposition in the 1440s by the literary elite and Korean Confucian scholars. They believed Chinese writing was the only legitimate system, and saw Hangul as a threat to their status.

OCT 9

1446

PUBLICATION OF
훈민정음 HUN MIN JEONG EUM

"The Proper Sounds
for the Instruction of the People"

OCT 9 became Hangul Day,
a national holiday, in South Korea

나랏말ᄊᆞ미
中듕國귁에달아
文문字ᄍᆞ와로서르ᄉᆞᄆᆞᆺ디아니ᄒᆞᆯᄊᆡ
이런젼ᄎᆞ로어린百ᄇᆡᆨ姓셩이
니르고져홇배이셔도
ᄆᆞᄎᆞᆷ내제ᄠᅳ들시러펴디
몯ᄒᆞᇙ노미하니라
내이ᄅᆞᆯ爲윙ᄒᆞ야어엿비너겨
새로스믈여듧字ᄍᆞᄅᆞᆯᄆᆡᇰᄀᆞ노니
사ᄅᆞᆷ마다ᄒᆡᅇᅧ수ᄫᅵ니겨날로ᄡᅮ
메便뼌安ᅙᅡᆫ킈ᄒᆞ고져ᄒᆞᇙᄯᆞᄅᆞ미니라

After the Japanese conquest, which occurred in 1910, Japanese was made the official language of Korea. However, the Korean alphabet was still taught in Korean-established schools built after the annexation. Japan banned earlier Korean literature from public schooling, which became mandatory for children, as well as from schools in 1938 as part of a policy of cultural assimilation, and all Korean-language publications were outlawed in 1941.

97.9%

total population of age 15 and over can read and write ; male: 99.2% ; female: 96.6% (2002) (source: CIA)

UNESCO KING SEJONG LITERACY PRIZE

an annual prize awarded to two institutions, organizations or individuals "for their contribution to the fight against illiteracy."

source: wikipedia.org/hangul

Consonant	Name	Pronunciation
ㄱ	gi-yŏk	g (k)
ㄴ	ni-ŭn	n (n)
ㄷ	di-gŭt	d (t)
ㄹ	ri-ŭl	r (l)
ㅁ	mi-ŭm	m (m)
ㅂ	bi-up	b (p)
ㅅ	shi-ot	s (t)
ㅇ	i-ŭng	silent (ng)
ㅈ	ji-ŭt	j (t)
ㅊ	chi-ŭt	ch (t)
ㅋ	ki-ŭk	k (k)
ㅌ	ti-ŭt	t (t)
ㅍ	pi-ŭp	p (p)
ㅎ	hi-ŭt	h (t)

ㄲ	ssang gi-yŏk	gg (k)
ㄸ	ssang di-gŭt	tt (t)
ㅃ	ssang bi-ŭp	bb (p)
ㅆ	ssang shi-ot	ss (t)
ㅉ	ssang ji-ŭt	ch (t)

Korean alphabet consists of 14 consonants and 10 vowels.

The ones in gray are special ones - these consonants are called **tense consonants**, and are said with a harder, stiffer sound.

And the vowels in gray are called **diphthongs**, or **complex vowels**, meaning "double vowels".

They are made up of two vowels to create one sound.

Keep in mind that there are no English/Roman letters that perfectly describe the sounds.

But don't worry - listen to the audio files and keep practicing and you will start hearing the differences!

Vowel Pronunciation			
ㅏ	a	ㅐ	ae
ㅑ	ya	ㅒ	yae
ㅓ	ŏ	ㅔ	e
ㅕ	yŏ	ㅖ	ye
ㅗ	o	ㅚ	oe
ㅛ	yo	ㅟ	wi
ㅜ	u	ㅢ	ŭi
ㅠ	yu	ㅘ	wa
ㅡ	ŭ	ㅝ	wŏ
ㅣ	i	ㅙ	wae
		ㅞ	we

And the sounds in parenthesis represent their usage as a **final consonant**, or **batchim**.

Little confusing? Don't worry! We will cover this in more detail later.

Korean alphabets are then put together to create a **syllable block**, which is composed of a **beginning consonant**, a **middle/final vowel**, and an **optional final consonant**, known as **batchim**. In order to create a syllable block, you need at least one consonant and one vowel. Let's take a look at the example below.

나 무

na   mu

Here is an example.

나무 (na mu), meaning "tree".
Let's look at how the word is structured.

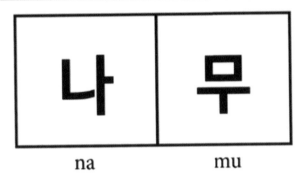

consonant

vowel

As you can see, a syllable block is composed of a consonant and a vowel. At this point, you might have noticed the position of a vowel is different on the two syllables.

ㄴ ㅏ
n   a

consonant   vowel

ㅏ	ㅑ	ㅓ	ㅕ	ㅐ	ㅣ	ㅒ	ㅔ	ㅖ
아	야	어	여	애	이	얘	에	예

The 9 vowels above are positioned **to the right side of** a consonant.
When a vowel is spoken by itself, ㅇ, which is silent, is always placed as a place holder.

ㅗ	ㅛ	ㅜ	ㅠ	ㅡ	ㅚ	ㅟ	ㅢ	ㅘ	ㅝ	ㅙ	ㅞ
오	요	우	유	으	외	위	의	와	워	왜	웨

The 12 vowels above are positioned **below** a consonant. Just try to memorize them for now.

As promised, let's talk about **final consonants**, or **batchim.** Simply put, they are the very last consonant character of a word ending in a consonant. For example, the word **"good"** has a final consonant of **"d"**, while the word **"Korean"** has a final consonant of **"n"**. The word **"language"**, however, **does not** have a final consonant because it ends with a vowel. Korean is just the same. See the following to understand better.

consonant

vowel

final consonant

ggum
("dream")

As you can see, the ㅁ comes at the bottom to serve as a final consonant. Notice the vowel ㅜ is placed underneath the consonant ㄲ.

This is the rule we learned just a page ago ;)

Let's take a look at another example to practice.

bap
("meal")

consonant   vowel

final consonant

In this case, the vowel ㅏ is placed to the right side of a consonant ㅂ, and the final consonant ㅂ is placed underneath the vowel. This is what it looks like.

It's easier to remember like this : **the final consonant is always placed underneath a vowel**, whether the vowel is the right side-type vowel or the underneath type-vowel. Oh, and the word **batchim** literally means "to support/ hold up", so just picture it holding a consonant and a vowel ;)

so
("cow")

consonant

vowel

As a reminder, a syllable that ends in a vowel alone **does not need a final consonant, or batchim.**

top 10

all-time popular Korean foods

01 비빔밥 [bi-bim-bap]
Rice Mixed with Vegetables and Beef

Rice topped with various cooked vegetables, such as zucchini, mushrooms and bean sprouts, plus beef and a fried egg. Served with red chili paste, which should be mixed in thoroughly.

02 냉면 [naeng-myeon]
Chilled Buckwheat Noodle Soup

Noodles made with buckwheat and starch. Served in a chilled beef broth with pickled radish, sliced Korean pear and a hard-boiled egg. It is often served with a side dish of vinegar and mustard.

03 삼계탕 [sam-gye-tang]
Ginseng Chicken Soup

Whole young chicken stuffed with ginseng, sticky rice, Korean dates and garlic. It is widely recognized as an energy- boosting meal during summer.

04 불고기 [bul-go-gi]
Grilled or Roasted Marinated Beef.

Thin slices of beef, marinated in a soy sauce, and usually grilled at the table.

05 떡볶이 [tteok-bok-ki]
Stir-Fried Rice Cake

A Korean dish that is stir-fried with rice cake, vegetables and fish cake in a spicy sauce.

06 삼겹살 [sam-gyeop-sal]
Korean-Style Bacon

Rashers of bacon, grilled at the table and dipped in a mixture of sesame oil and salt.

07 김밥 [kim-bap]
Dried Seaweed Rolls(Korean Rolls)

Vegetables and cooked egg are placed on seasoned rice. The ingredients are then rolled in dried seaweed and sliced into bite-sized pieces.

08 김치 [kim-chi]
Salted and Fermented Vegetables

Cured and fermented vegetables, usually Napa cabbage, mixed with julienned white radish, leek, garlic, ginger, red chili powder, salt and fish sauce. This is the most common kind of kimchi.

09 순두부찌개 [sun-du-bu-jji-gae]
Spicy Soft Tofu Stew

Spicy stew containing soft tofu, seafood, and sometimes egg. It is served piping hot in an earthenware pot.

10 빙수 [bing-su]
Shaved Ice

Ice shavings and various ingredients such as sweetened condensed milk, fruit syrups, various fruits such as strawberries, kiwifruit, and bananas, small pieces of tteok (rice cake), chewy jelly bits, and cereal flakes. It is often topped with ice cream or frozen yogurt.

the evolution of KIMCHI

Korean people and Kimchi go WAY BACK
Kimchi is an inseparable part of the Korean lifestyle,
to the point where they view it as part of their identity.
(Heck, it even has "KIM" in it.)

Three Kingdom Period (57 BC to 668 AD)

Pickled Vegetables
In its primitive form as pickled vegetables optimized for long term storage

People called it "ji", meaning "pickeld vegetables"

Joseon Dynasty (1392 - 1892)

Gains Popularity
Around 16th century, the name "timchae" first appears. It is speculated that it came from the word "chimchae" which means "submerging vegetables under (salt) water"

Eventually it becomes "kimchi" through palatalization

김치

Japanese Invasion (1592 - 1598)

Introduction of Chili
The Japanese brought this now-essential-staple-of-Korean-food with them during their failed invasion a-ttempts. It was, however, considered toxic for about 200 years and couldn't earn a spot in the kitchen

Yes. Kimchi used to be WHITE

Modern Day Korea (Early 1900's)

Tong Baechu Kimchi Invented
With the GENIUS invention of "tong baechu (whole cabbage)" Kimchi in the early 1900's, it started to look like the one we see today

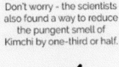

Until this point, RADISH was the most popular ingredient used

Future of Kimchi (2008)

Kimchi to Space!
South Korean scientists created a special low-calorie, vitamin-rich, and bacteria-free (although on earth they are essential for the fermentation to take place, but they feared that cosmic rays might mutate them) "Space Kimchi". And South Korea's very first astro-naut, Yi So-yeon, took it to space with her.

Don't worry - the scientists also found a way to reduce the pungent smell of Kimchi by one-third or half.

THE STORY BEHIND
KOREAN LAST NAMES

10 MOST COMMON LAST NAMES

김KIM (21.8%)

이LEE (14.8%)

박PARK (8.5%)

최CHOI (4.7%)

정JUNG (4.4%)

강KANG (2.3%)

조CHO (2.1%)

윤YOON (2.1%)

장JANG (2.0%)

임LIM (1.7%)

SOURCE: STATISTICS KOREA (2000)

THERE ARE A TOTAL OF
286
LAST NAMES IN KOREA

Another interesting characteristic is that most of the Korean names are composed of three syllables. For one-syllable last names such as Kim, Lee, and Park, they are followed by two-syllable first names such as Min Ho, Ji Hoon, and Young Soo. For double-syllable last names (not that many) such as Namkung, Jegal, and Sunwoo, one-syllable first names such as are commonly given. Of course, there are quite a lot of people with a two-syllable last name with a a two-syllable first name, making it a four-syllable name.

Q: WITH ONLY 286 LAST NAMES, ARE ALL KOREANS RELATED?

Thanks to 본관 (bon gwan) - the birthplace of the first ancestor or founder of the family name (there are some 4,179 of them present today), one family clan can be distinguished from one another (e.g., Gyungju Kim, Seoul Kim, Pyongyang Kim, oh what the heck, New York Kim).

KOREAN SUPERSTITIONS

THAT MANY PEOPLE STILL BELIEVE

LAYING DOWN RIGHT AFTER A MEAL = YOU BECOME A COW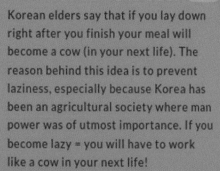

Korean elders say that if you lay down right after you finish your meal will become a cow (in your next life). The reason behind this idea is to prevent laziness, especially because Korea has been an agricultural society where man power was of utmost importance. If you become lazy = you will have to work like a cow in your next life!

YOU'LL DIE IF YOU WRITE YOUR NAME IN RED INK

There are many theories as to why this is prohibited : 1) red = death, as it's the same color as blood. 2) When Grand Prince Suyang of the Joseon Dynasty was plotting a coup, he used red ink to make a hit list of enemies. 3) During the Korean War, red ink was used to cross out the names of the killed.

STICKING CHOPSTICKS STRAIGHT INTO RICE

This is also a big no-no in Korean culture because doing this resembles what happens at a Korean funeral ceremony.

NUMBER 4 = DEATH

The Korean word for number 4 is "sa", which is pronounced the same as the Chinese word "death". For this reason, number 4 is often skipped/omitted in elevators and other places, or replaced with "F", just like number 13 in the Western culture.

GIFTING SHOES TO YOUR SIGNIFICANT OTHER = HE/SHE WILL RUN AWAY

While it sounds silly, many Korean couples have a strong belief that gifting shoes to someone you love will make them run away from you! Another related expression is "putting on rubber shoes the other way around" It's an idiomatic expressions used to describe how a girl dumps her boyfriend or cheats on him while he's serving in the military. Rubber shoes were the most popular type of shoes girls used to wear back in the old days, and wearing them the other way around symbolizes change of heart.

HAVING A PIG DREAM = GOOD FORTUNE COMING YOUR WAY

Pig is a symbol of prosperity, and Korean people believe that having a dream of a pig is indicative of something good, especially wealth and prosperity, is coming your way. For that reason, the first thing any Korean would do after having a dream of a pig is buying a lottery ticket, and there are countless cases where lottery winners say the reason they bought a ticket was because of a pig dream!

KOREAN TAFFY "YEOT" WILL MAKE YOU PASS THE NEXT BIG EXAM

What's the hottest item among Korean students preparing for a big exam? It's the Korean taffy, or "yeot (엿)". The belief comes from the fact that Korean expression of "passing a test" is translated as "sticking (to the group of "test-passers". By the same logic, Korean rice cake, "tteok (떡)", is another popular item due to its stickiness.

WALKING DOWN ALONG THE "DEOK SU GUNG STONE WALL" WILL MAKE COUPLES BREAK UP

There's one place in Seoul which you should avoid visiting with your significant other - it's the 덕수궁 돌담길 (deok su gung dol dam gil), a stone wall surrounding the Deok Su Gung Royal Palace. There's this urban legend/myth that says walking down along the wall will make couples break up. The origin of this belief is unclear, but there IS the Seoul Family Court right nearby. Which might explain the idea.

DO YOU BELIEVE IN THESE IDEAS?

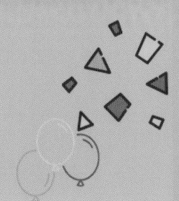

dol jabi 돌잡이

PREDICTING BABY'S FUTURE

origin

In the past, the mortality rates for Korean children were quite high and many children died before their first birthday

For this reason, first birthday has always been an important milestone for a baby and parents.

The whole village used to celebrate a baby's first birthday, sharing food and wishing for long life and fortune for the baby.

what is dol jabi?

> "Dol" 돌 means "anniversary" or "birthday".

> For babies, "dol" usually means "first birthday".

> "Jabi" 잡이 literally means "to grab"

> "Dol jabi" literally means "to grab at the first birthday"

> It's a traditional ceremonial event with a belief that whatever the baby picks off the table, among many items presented, predicts baby's fortune/future!

meaning (some of them are traditional, and some are new, reflecting change of trend)

thread
"longevity"

bow & arrow
"military figure"

book
"scholar"

money
"wealth"

grapes
"fecundity"

rice
"prosperity"

ruler
"architect"

stethoscope
"medical doctor"

ball
"athlete"

gavel
"judge"

keyboard
"programmer"

microphone
"entertainer"

needle
"dexterity"

pencil
"writer"

KOREAN
BLOOD TYPE PERSONALITY THEORY

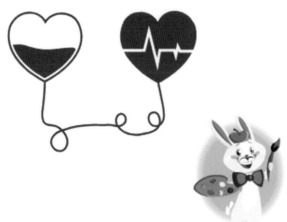

BLOOD TYPE A
INTROVERTED PERFECTIONIST

- Conservative/Introverted
- Find difficulty in expressing emotions / trusting others
- Quite shy in front of strangers
- Often called a fundamentalist and a perfectionist
- Have a strong sense of responsibility at work, and easily gain the trust of the organization
- Always make plans with extreme caution, but often seen as lacking flexibility
- Look like a hard worker, but you can be a party animal in disguise
- Can be quite adventurous when dating

BLOOD TYPE B
CREATIVE AND (TOO) CURIOUS

- Inquisitive / Full of curiosity
- Have an endless stock of topics for conversation
- Full of original ideas - exceptional ability in project planning
- Have a strong interest in new things and often have trouble focusing
- Sometimes called inconsistent
- Prefer working at own pace (freelancer) than in organizational settings
- Compassionate and tender-hearted - considerate of other's feelings, but sometimes seen as too nosy

BLOOD TYPE O
COMPETITIVE LEADER

- Personality - Warm-hearted / Behavior - Goal-oriented
- Not bothered by minor obstacles and have the ability to focus on given tasks
- Strong sense of comradeship, often assume the leadership role within a group
- Often seen as a romanticist pursuing dreams, but can be surprisingly cool-headed in pressing situations
- Hate losing and competitive - can be seen as condescending and self-complacent

BLOOD TYPE AB
MYSTERIOUS AMPHIBIAN

- Unpredictable - different characteristics depending on which side of the A&B combination gets ignited
- Superb ability to adapt to any given situation
- Objective in making decisions, thus less prone to making mistakes
- Often seen as someone who's easily led, but also can be wishy-washy
- Prefer to keep personal life private and don't care much about those of others, either

BTW, HOW (IN)ACCURATE ARE THEY?

The Korean Society of Hematology officially announced that there is absolutely no scientific basis for this belief and personality is a byproduct of environmental factors such as family and education

Guardians of Korean Villages

Hi there! We are called 장승 jang seung, and you've probably seen us in Korean historical dramas, standing tall at the entrance of a village, making scary faces! As you might have guessed, we are village guardians, or Korean totem poles, usually made of wood. Traditionally, we are seen at the edges of villages to mark the boundaries of a village, while serving a dual purpose of frightening away demons and evil spirits.

Homer Bezaleel Hulbert, an American Protestant missionary described us as "Village Devil Posts" in The Passing of Korea (1906).

We are usually adorned with engravings describing the characteristics of the carved figures along the front of the poles. "Male" jang seungs usually bear engravings in Hangul or Hanja reading "Great General of All Under Heaven," or cheon-ha-dae-jang-gun 천하대장군 天下大將軍 and are decorated with headpieces resembling those worn by Korean aristocrats or scholars. "Female" jang seungs, on the other hand, wear less elaborate headpieces and usually bear engravings reading "Female General of the Underworld," or ji-ha-yeo-jang-gun 지하여장군 地下女將軍

When you visit Korea, don't be intimated by our scary looks because we're friendly and love tourists!

Did you know that Korea has more than 40% of the world's dolmen, which are mostly concentrated in these three sites : Gochang, Hwasun, and Ganghwa. UNESCO designated these places as World Heritage Site in 2000, and they are believed to be used as grave markers and for ritual purposes, during the first millennium BCE. This is when the Megalithic (large stones) Culture was prominent on the Korean Peninsula.

These dolmens are believed to mark the graves of the ruling elite, and what makes them more valuable is that a lot of artifacts such as pottery, comma-shaped jewels, bronzes, and stone tools have been excavated from these dolmen.

When a group of dolmens are found, there is usually a uniquely large dolmen, also different in direction than other dolmens. Although no written records are available, it's presumed to be a simple function that was built to display the authority and prestige of the tomb-building group.

Gojoseon, Korea's First Nation (2333 BC ~ 108 BC)

According to the founding legend recorded in the Samguk Yusa (record of history and legends), the Lord of Heaven, 환인 Hwanin had a son, 환웅 Hwanung, who descended to Baekdu Mountain (the highest in Korean peninsula) and founded the city of 신시 Shinsi. Then a tiger and a bear came to Hwanung and asked how they could become human beings and they were told that if they went into a cave and lived there for 100 days while only eating mugwort and garlic Hwanung will transform them into human beings. Both accepted the challenge, but about halfway through the 100 days the tiger gave up and ran out of the cave. The bear, on the other hand, successfully restrained herself and became a beautiful woman called Ungnyeo (웅녀, 熊女). Hwanung married Ungnyeo, and she gave birth to Dangun, who becomes the founding father of 고조선 Gojoseon in 2333 BC. Today, the said legend is interpreted by scholars as a symbolic representation of a marriage with a member of a bear-worshiping tribe, rather than a literal bear-turned-human woman. The founding date, or 개천절 *gae cheon jeol* ("the heaven opening day") is celebrated as a national holiday in Korea (October 3rd).

Dangun Wangeom

3 Three Kingdoms Period (57 BC ~ 668)

57 BC   **Bak Hyeokgeose** founds **Silla**

37 BC   **Jumong** founds **Goguryeo**

18 BC   **Onjo** founds **Baekje**

372   Under **Sosurim**, **Goguryeo** imports **Buddhism** from Former **Qin of China.**

384   **Chimnyu** of Baekje officially adopts **Buddhism.**

392   **Gwanggaeto the Great** of Goguryeo begins his reign, expanding Goguryeo into a major regional power.

433   **Baekje** and **Silla form an alliance** against Goguryeo's aggression.

527   **Silla** formally adopts **Buddhism / Martyrdom of Ichadon**

553   **Silla** attacks Baekje, **breaking the alliance.**

598   **Sui Dynasty** attacks Goguryeo and **Goguryeo-Sui War** begins

612   **Goguryeo repulses** second Sui invasion at **the Salsu.**

614   **Sui Dynasty defeated.**

645   First campaign in the **Goguryeo–Tang War.**

648   **Silla** establishes **alliance** with **Tang.**

660   **Baekje falls** to the **Silla-Tang** forces.

668   **Goguryeo falls** to the **Silla-Tang** forces.

The map of history of Korea in 476, the moment of greatest territorial expansion of Goguryeo.
(Wikimedia Commons)

Unified Silla 통일신라 (676 ~ 935)

676 **Silla repels Chinese alliance** forces from Korean peninsula, **completes unification** of much of the Three Kingdoms.

698 The founding of **Balhae** by former **Goguryeo** general **Dae Joyeong**.

751 **Silla**, at its cultural peak, constructs **Seokguram** and **Bulguksa**.

828 **Jang Bogo** establishes **Cheonghaejin**, a **major center of trade with China, Japan, and Vietnam**.

918 **Founding** of **Goryeo** by **Taejo** of Goryeo.

935 **Silla** formally **surrenders** to **Goryeo**, Goryeo controls the Korean peninsula.

신라 Silla, the Golden Kingdom (57 BC ~ 935)

Golden Crowns of Silla, found in Chunmachong. National Treasures of Korea No. 188

Silla, believed to have been founded by Bak Hyeok Geo Se in 57 BC, was one of the three kingdoms of ancient Korea. Silla developed into a full-fledged kingdom as a result of the establishment of the hereditary monarchy of the Kim family. During this time, Buddhism was adopted as the national religion and it flourished. The traces – magnificent Buddha sculptures and temples can be found everywhere in Gyeongju, where the kingdom's capital was located. The people of Shilla, especially the aristocrats, were fond of extravagant luxury. Among all, gold ornaments, such as gold crowns, belts, and various jewelry show how dexterous and artsy they were! No wonder they are called "The Golden Kingdom".

고구려 Goguryeo, the Largest Dynasty in Korean History (37 BC ~ 668)

Goguryeo is said to have been founded by Jumong in 37 BCE, and was the largest of the three kingdoms, which became a full-fledged aristocratic state during the reign of King Sosurim, who promulgated various laws and decrees that helped centralizing royal authority. Like other ancient Korean kingdoms, Buddhism was the cultural backbone, while Confucian education was emphasized as a means of regulating/managing the social order. Today, some of the ruins and tombs, which became UNESCO World Heritage sites in 2004, can be found in the far southern Jilin province in China, where the kingdom's territory covered.

Tomb of the Hunters, Goguryeo mural, South Pyongan Province, North Korea

백제 Baekje, the Cultural Powerhouse (18 BC ~ 660)

Gilt Bronze Buddha from the Baekje Kingdom that was unearthed in Buyeo, South Chungcheong Province, in 1907

Baekje is traditionally said to have been founded by a legendary leader Onjo in 18 BC in the Kwangju area. Around the 3rd century AD, it became a fully-developed kingdom, during the reign of King Goi, and during the reign of King Geunchogo, it ruled a significant portion of central Korea, including the whole Han River basin. Buddhism and Confucianism were the two pillars of the kingdom, and a large number of eminent scholars were produced. One of the most famous and distinctive artwork of the era is a Buddha statue that has a subtle and mysterious smile, known as the "Baekje Smile".

박혁거세 Bak Hyeokgeose

He was the founding monarch of Silla and the progenitor of all Bak (Park) clans in Korea. 赫 hyeok, means "bright, radiant, glowing", 居 geo, means "live, dwell,", 世 se, means "generation; world;". According to the Samguk Yusa (a collection of legends, folktales and historical accounts relating to the Three Kingdoms of Korea), leaders of chiefdoms (believed to have been refugees from Gojoseon) got together to discuss selecting a king and forming a kingdom, and right that moment in the forest, a strange light shone from the sky, and where a white horse bowed down, there was a large egg from which a boy came out of. After getting bathed, his body radiated and beasts jumped with joy. The people revered him, and made him king of the state named Seorabeol when he became 13. He married Lady Aryeong, who is said to have been born from the ribs of a dragon. The Park clans are the third largest group in Korea today.

주몽 / 동명성왕 Jumong / Dong Myeong Seong Wang

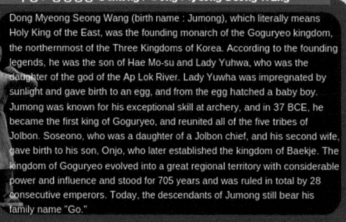

Dong Myeong Seong Wang (birth name : Jumong), which literally means Holy King of the East, was the founding monarch of the Goguryeo kingdom, the northernmost of the Three Kingdoms of Korea. According to the founding legends, he was the son of Hae Mo-su and Lady Yuhwa, who was the daughter of the god of the Ap Lok River. Lady Yuwha was impregnated by sunlight and gave birth to an egg, and from the egg hatched a baby boy. Jumong was known for his exceptional skill at archery, and in 37 BCE, he became the first king of Goguryeo, and reunited all of the five tribes of Jolbon. Soseono, who was a daughter of a Jolbon chief, and his second wife, gave birth to his son, Onjo, who later established the kingdom of Baekje. The kingdom of Goguryeo evolved into a great regional territory with considerable power and influence and stood for 705 years and was ruled in total by 28 consecutive emperors. Today, the descendants of Jumong still bear his family name "Go."

온조 Onjo

Onjo, the son of Jumong and Soseono of the Goguryeo Kingdom, was the founding monarch of Baekje which was located in the western part of the Korean peninsula. According to the Samguk Sagi (a historical record of the Three Kingdoms of Korea), he was the ancestor of all Baekje kings. He was the younger brother of Yuri, who became Goguryeo's second king, and younger brother of Biryu who built small state in Michuhol. When Biryu died, his people joined Sipje, which Onjo later renamed to Baekje. Onjo was able to successfully manage and stifle sporadic rebellions from other tribes, and reigned for 46 years, and laid the foundations for a powerful dynasty that would last for 678 years and 31 rulers.

광개토대왕 Gwang Gae To the Great

Gwanggaeto the Great (birth name: Go Damdeok 고담덕), was the nineteenth monarch of Goguryeo Kingdom. His full posthumous name can be translated as "Entombed in Gukgangsang, Broad Expander of Domain, Peacemaker, Supreme King". Under Gwanggaeto, Goguryeo rose as a powerful empire in East Asia, making enormous advances and conquests into western Manchuria against Khitan tribes; inner Mongolia and the Maritime Province of Russia against numerous nations and tribes, as well as the Han River valley in central Korea to control over two-thirds of the Korean peninsula. He also defeated Baekje, which was the then most powerful kingdom of Korea. His accomplishments are recorded on the Gwanggaeto Stele, erected in 414 at the supposed site of his tomb in Jian, present-day China–North Korea border, and is still standing tall as the largest engraved steel in the world.

Martyrdom of Ichadon

Ichadon 이차돈 (501-527) was a Buddhist monk and advisor to the Silla king Beopheung, who desired to promulgate Buddhism as the state religion, but was facing opposition from the court officials. Ichadon devised a strategy to overcome the opposition, convincing the king to make such proclamation using the royal seal. Ichadon told the king to deny having made such a proclamation, and Ichadon would confess and accept the punishment of execution for forgery. He prophesied to the king that at his execution a miracle would convince the opposing court faction. His scheme went as planned, and when he was executed, the earth shook, the sun was darkened, beautiful flowers rained from the sky, and white blood instead of red blood sprayed 100 feet in the air from his beheaded corpse. The omen was accepted as a manifestation of heaven's approval, making Buddhism the state religion in 527 CE. His body was then taken to the sacred Geumgang mountains and buried there with respect. His martyrdom led to the construction of Heungryun monastery, Silla's first state-sponsored temple.

Battle of Salsu 살수대첩

Recorded as one of the most lethal battles in world history, it was an enormous victory by Goguryeo over the Sui Dynasty of China. Led by General Eulji Mundeok, lured the Sui army into the Salsu River, where he prepared an attack. He cut off the flow of water with a dam in advance, and opened it when the unsuspecting Sui troops were halfway across. Thousands drowned and the surviving troops were killed by the Guguryeo cavalry. Over 300,000 Sui troops died while only 2,700 troops were lost on Guguryeo's side. This defeat had a major impact on the Sui Dynasty, causing them to collapse from within, leading to an eventual fall.

Great Gilt-bronze Incense Burner

"One of the crowning excavation achievements in the past century, the Baekje Gilt-Bronze Incense Burner, 백제 금동대향로 *baekje geumdong dae hyang ro* gave a critical turning point to the studies in the Baekje Dynasty history. The Burner embraces the mind of the Baekje people who delicately chased their ideal world with exquisite techniques and high appreciative eyes. The Incense Burner of this kind has been found anywhere in the world since then. It is no wonder that it can be really called a masterpiece", (Chungnam.Net Media). It uses realism and is three-dimensional, and the dragon and phoenix symbolize a yin and yang motif, and others also think it incorporates Buddhist and Taoist themes. The uniqueness of the artifact suggests that the burner may have been used for ancestral rites or other unique ceremonies. It measures 64 centimeters in height, the body is 19 centimeters in diameter, and weighs 11.8 kilograms. It's estimated to have been made in the 6th century.

Golden Crowns, found in Chunmachong

The Gold Crown is believed to be the crown of King Soji or King Jijeung, and was excavated from *Cheonmachong* 천마총 (Tomb No. 155, also known as "The Heavenly Horse Tomb") in 1973, and is currently housed in Gyeongju National Museum after getting designated as the 188th National Treasure of Korea. The crown is 32.5 centimeters in height, and there are three prongs forming the Chinese character 山 "mountain" on the front of the crown. On the back, there are two prongs in the shape of a deer antler. There are also two dangling gold chains, hanging from the end of the headband, shaped as leaves.

Gilt-bronze Maitreya in Meditation

It's believed to be a statue of the Maitreya, the future Buddha, in a semi-seated contemplative pose, commonly referred to as the Contemplative Bodhisattva, Pensive Bodhisattva, or Gilt-Bronze Seated Maitreya in English. In Korean it is frequently referred to as *bangasayusang* 반가사유상 (National Treasure of Korea No. 83.) It's recognized as one of the finest Buddhist sculptures ever produced, and it's currently housed at the National Museum of Korea and is one of the most popular exhibits there. The bodhisattva is seated on a stool with his right leg crossed over his left knee, while a finger rests subtly on his face, with a thoughtful expression. The pose itself, symbolizes an event occurred during Buddha's life before his renouncement as a prince: While observing farmers till the fields, he awakened to the cyclical nature of human suffering, and the artwork depict the posture at this moment of awakening.

The Smile of Silla Roof-End Tile

A roof-end tile with a human face, well known as "The Smile of Silla," was excavated on the site where Yeongmyosa 영묘사 Temple stood during the Japanese colonial era. This hand-crafted title, called "Sumakse (수막세)" in Korean, attached to a curved tile at the edges of a roof/wall. Contrary to other cultures where scary faces are used (e.g., goblins), the people of Silla instead used friendly smiles to soothe all bad spirits and send them back to where they originally came from.

석굴암 Seok Gu Ram

The Seokguram Grotto (man-made cave) is part of the Bulguksa Temple complex, which measures four kilometers along the east of the temple on Toham Mountain, in Gyeongju, South Korea. This hermitage has been classified as National Treasure No. 24 in 1962, and was added to the UNESCO World Heritage in 1995, along with the Bulguksa Temple complex. The grotto is situated to overlook the East Sea and rests 750 meters above sea level. It's said to have been built by Kim Daeseong and originally called Seokbulsa ("Stone Buddha Temple") whose construction first took place in 742 when he resigned his position in the king's court in 751 during the reign of King Gyeongdeok of Silla, which is considered as the cultural peak of the kingdom. According to a legend, Kim dedicated the Grotto to his parents from a previous life, and the Temple to his parents in his present life. The construction was finished in 774, and is acknowledged as one of the finest Buddhist sculptures in the world, and is currently one of the best known cultural destinations in South Korea.

Goryeo, the Glory of Korea (918~1388)

918 Founding of Goryeo by **Taejo**.

1033 Goryeo builds the **Cheonri Jangseong (lit. "Thousand Li Wall")**, a massive wall running along the northern border.

1145 **Kim Bu-sik** compiles the **Samguk Sagi**, Korea's oldest extant history text.

1231 The **Mongol invasions** of Korea begin.

1234 **Choi Yun-ui**'s **Sangjeong Gogeum Yemun** is published, world's first metal-block printed text.

1251 Goryeo completes the **Tripitaka Koreana**, the most comprehensive and oldest intact version of the Buddhist canon in Chinese script.

1270 Goryeo signs a **peace treaty with the Mongols**, beginning an 80-year period of Yuan overlordship. The **Sambyeolcho Rebellion** lasts for three more years.

1285 **Il-yeon** compiles the **Samguk Yusa**, record of history and legends.

1388 **General Yi Seonggye**, ordered to engage China in a border dispute, **turns his troops against the Goryeo court**.

Did You Know?

The name "Korea" comes from 고려 Goryeo, which was the name given to the dynasty established by General Wang Geon in AD 918. Goryeo means "high and clear." Some poetic interpretations of the name Korea are "Land of High Mountains and Sparkling Streams" and "Land of the Morning Calm."

Red: Goguryeo's Cheolli Jangseong.
Blue: Goryeo's Cheolli Jangseong.

팔만대장경 Pal Man Dae Jang Gyeong / Tripitaka Koreana

The Tripiṭaka Koreana or Palman Daejanggyeong ("Eighty-Thousand Tripiṭaka") is a compilation of the Buddhist scriptures, carved onto 81,258 wooden printing blocks in the 13th century. According to the records, the work began in 1011 during the Goryeo–Khitan War and was completed in 1087. During the wartime, Goryeo believed the act of carving the scriptures onto the woodblocks would bring about a divine intervention (i.e., Buddha's help), which would help the kingdom persevere through the difficult times. The original Triptaka Koreana contained around 6,000 volumes, but they were destroyed by fire during the Mongol invasions of Korea in 1232. Seeking divine assistance once again with fighting the Mongols, King Gojong ordered the revision and re-creation of the Tripiṭaka, and the carving began in 1237. and was completed after 12 years, and the result is just beyond anyone's imagination – it's the world's most comprehensive and oldest intact version of Buddhist canon in Hanja (Chinese Characters incorporated into Korean language) scrip. Surprisingly, of the 52,330,152 characters carved, there are no known errors or errata found. Each wood block is 24 centimeters high and 70 centimeters long, as thick as 4 centimeters. With over 1,496 titles and 6,568 volumes, they weigh 280 tons total. The most amazing part is they still remain in pristine condition – no warping/deformation despite it's been over 750 years since creation, thanks to the special treatment the craftsmen incorporated. The production of the Tripiṭaka Koreana is a symbol of national commitment and desire to fight off the invaders. For that reason, it was designated as Korea's National Treasure in 1962, and was inscribed in the UNESCO Memory of the World Register in 2007. Currently, it's stored in Haeinsa, a Buddhist temple in South Gyeongsang Province, in South Korea.

태조 Tae Jo of Gogryeo

태조 Taejo (r. 918-943 CE, birth name 왕건 Wang Geon), was the founder and first king of the Goryeo kingdom which unified and ruled ancient Three Kingdoms of Korea from 918 CE to 1392 CE. The posthumous title, Taejo means 'Great Founder', and he laid the foundation stones for his dynasty which witnessed unprecedented flourishing of Korean culture. The Unified Silla Kingdom (668-935 CE) ruled over the Korean peninsula for nearly three centuries, but started to decline as rebellions broke out frequently from the peasantry and the aristocracy. During the time, 견훤 Gyeon Hwon, a peasant leader, rose to power amid the political turmoil in 892 CE and revived the old Baekje kingdom. A little later in 901 CE, 궁예 Gung Ye, an aristocratic Buddhist monk leader who was supported by his first minister and general Wang Geon, proclaimed a new Guguryeo state. Wang Geon succeeded Gung Ye, who was killed by the hands of his people due to his fanatical tyranny, in 918 CE. Wang Geon attacked Later Baekje, founded by Gyeon Hwon, and the declining Silla. In 935 CE, Silla finally surrendered and Wang Geon unified the kingdoms once again, under a new name, 고려 Goryeo ("High and Beautiful"), whose name implies that it's the successor of the previous kingdom, Goguryeo. He kept a large portion of the Silla institutions of government, and distributed lands and high government positions to former Baekje and Silla elites. He also continued his endorsement of Buddhism and Confucianism.

삼국사기 Sam Guk Sa Gi and 삼국유사 Sam Guk Yu Sa

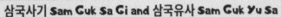

The Samguk Sagi, literally meaning 'History of the Three Kingdoms', is a collection of historical records of the three ancient kingdoms (1st century BCE ~ 7th century CE Goguryeo, Baekje, Silla). It's the oldest surviving chronicle of Korean history, and the compilation project was ordered by King Injong of Goryeo and was undertaken by the government official and historian 김부식 Kim Busik and a team of junior scholars. The project was completed in 1145. There are two clear motives for the project : One was to close the wide gap in knowledge concerning Korea's Three Kingdoms Era, as each of the three kingdoms had produced their own histories, which were mostly lost in the continual wars, and the dispersal of records of the fallen kingdoms. The other motive was to create a history with a purpose of educating Korean literati in their native history, while providing them with Korean exemplars of Confucian virtues, with a belief that history can guide the present while offering valuable lessons on good government and moral conduct. This was especially important because the dominant ideology of Goguryeo was Confucianism. Many scholars value the work for having made a profound impact on the concept of Korea and its people, and laid the foundation stones for Korean nationalism and identity, as it solely focused on the histories of the ancient Korean kingdoms, apart from the Chinese influence. The Samguk Yusa, literally meaning 'Memorabilia of the Three Kingdoms' is a compilation of the history and legends of Korea, starting all the way from the founding of the very first nation, Gojoseon, all the way up to the Three Kingdoms Period. Written by the Buddhist Monk 일연 Il Yeon, it differs from the Samguk Sagi as it covers various areas of history, with a focus on Buddhist legends and the folk tales of the Silla Dynasty, with a relatively smaller coverage on the other two kingdoms. Despite its limits, it remains today an invaluable historical source and component of Korean Literature.

Mongol Invasions and 삼별초 Sam Byeol Cho

Mongol Cavalry Men

From 1231, Goryeo was sporadically but continuously invaded by the Mongol Empire (1206~1388), who devastated a significant portion of the lands of Goryeo and its population throughout the series of invasions which lasted for nearly three decades (1231~1259). In order to escape from the attacks, the Goryeo government, controlled a the military regime led by the Choi family, decided to give up the land and flee to Gnaghwa Island, where the Mongolian horse riders were unable to land on, while having it as a resistance base against the Mongol invasion. Unfortunately, Goryeo had to face frequent rebellions from its own people, and struggle internally, mainly due to the fragile foundation of the government. In 1258, a large scale rebellion broke out and resulted in the establishment of Dongyeong Prefectures by the Mongols. Meanwhile, the Sambyeolcho (Three Elite Patrols), organized by the Choi clan to maintain order and security on the island base by performing roles as police and combat forces. Even after the Goryeo kingdom fell to the hands of the Mongols later, they continued to fight back tenaciously, moving bases multiples times, including Jindo and Jeju Island, but was eventually annihilated by the Mongol-Goryeo counter-insurgency troops on Jeju Island.

Joseon Dynasty, Land of Morning Calm (1392~1897)

1392 — **Yi Seonggye** is crowned king, officially beginning the Joseon Dynasty.

1396 — Capital moved to **Hanyang**. (modern day Seoul)

1402 — **Paper currency** initiated.

한글

1446 — The **Hangul alphabet**, created 3 years earlier, is promulgated by **King Sejong the Great**.

1592 — The **Japanese invasion** of Korea begins under the command of **Toyotomi Hideyoshi**. **Admiral Yi Sun-Sin** employs the **Turtle ship** to repel Japanese naval forces.

1653 — Dutch ship, with **Captain Hendrick Hamel**, wrecked on Jeju Island.

1791 — **Persecution of Catholicism** begins.

1864 — **Gojong** ascends the throne with his father, **Daewongun**, as Regent.

1866 — **French Campaign** against Korea.

1871 — **United States expedition** to Korea.

1876 — Korean ports are formally opened under the **Treaty of Ganghwa** with Imperial Japan.

1884 — **Kim Okgyun** leads the **Gapsin coup**. In 3 days, Chinese forces are able to overwhelm the Progressives and their Japanese supporters.

1894 — **Donghak Rebellion** prompts the First Sino-Japanese War and Gabo Reforms.

1895 — China recognizes Korean independence in the **Treaty of Shimonoseki**. **Empress Myeongseong** was murdered by Japanese assassins.

1896 — 11 February. **King Gojong** flees to the Russian legation in Korea (Seoul).

태조 / 이성계 Tae Jo / Yi Seong Gye

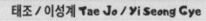

Tae Jo, whose birth name was Yi Seong Gye, was the founder and the first king of the Joseon Dynasty, reigning from 1392 to 1398, and was the main figure in overthrowing the Goryeo Dynasty. By the late 14th century, Goryeo Dynasty was beginning to fall apart, with its foundations collapsing from years of war against the Mongol Empire. During the time, then General Yi Seong-gye gained power and respect by pushing the Mongol remnants off the kingdom and repelling Japanese pirates. When the newly rising Ming Dynasty demanded the return of a significant portion of Goryeo's northern territory, Goryeo was split into two factions – anti-Ming who argued to fight back and those who seek peace. Yi, the latter, however, was chosen to lead the invasion. At Wihwa Island on the Amrok River, he decided to revolt and withdrew the troops, and headed back to the capital. The military coup succeeded, and he dethroned the King. He first put a puppet king, but later exiled him, and ascended the throne, and just like that the Joseon Dynasty era began

명성황후 Empress Myeong Seong

Empress Myeongseong was the first official wife of Gojong, the twenty-sixth king of Joseon and the first emperor of the Korean Empire. The government of Meiji Japan was ambitious with overseas expansion, and saw her as an obstacle, and put efforts to remove her, but failed. After the first Sino-Japanese War which ended with Japan's victory, Joseon came under the Japanese influence. As a result, the Empress argued for stronger ties between Korea and Russia as a means to bloc Japanese influence. The government of Meiji Japan considered Empress Myeongseong an obstacle to its overseas expansion. Efforts to remove her from the political arena, orchestrated through failed rebellions prompted by the father of King Gojong, the Heungseon Daewongun (an influential regent working with the Japanese), compelled her to take a harsher stand against Japanese influence. The Japanese government sent a group of ronins (assassins), and assassinated the Empress. This horrendous incident ignited outrage among other foreign powers, and the Joseon people's anti-Japanese sentiment soared.

창경궁 Chang Gyeong Gung

Changgyeonggung Palace, meaning "Magnificent Joy Palace" was constructed in 1483 by the ninth king of the Joseon Dynasty, King Seongjong, to take care of the wives of the preceding kings. Unlike other similar palaces, the size and structure is compact and simple. It's commonly referred to as "Donggwol," the "East Palace.", as it's connected with the Changdeokgung Palace on the east side. Sadly, most of the palace buildings were destroyed during the Japanese invasion of Korea in 1592. The main buildings such as Myeongjeongjeon, Munjeongjeon (council hall), Hwangyeongjeon (Hall), Inyangjeon (Hall), Gongsacheong, and Honghwamun (Gate), however, were rebuilt by the fifteenth king of the Joseon Dynasty, King Gwanghaegun. Later during the Japanese occupation (1910 – 1945), the Japanese built a zoo on the site and renamed the palace "Changgyeongwon," meaning "Changgyeong Garden." Since 1987, the palace has been reconstructed and much of its original form has been restored.

경복궁 Gyeong Bok Gung

Meaning ""Palace Greatly Blessed by Heaven", Gyeongbokgung Palace was the first and the largest of the royal palaces of the Joseon Dynasty. Built in 1395 at the heart of the newly selected capital Hanyang (modern day Seoul), it's also commonly referred to as the "Northern Palace" due to its location, which is furthest north from the neighboring places, and is considered by many as the most beautiful palaces. The palace has always been a symbol of the sovereignty of the Joseon Dynasty, and for that reason, there has been a tremendous effort in conserving it throughout history. During the Imjin War (Japanese Invasion 1592 – 15898), the palace was destroyed by fire, but was restored during the reign of King Gojong (1852 – 1919). After liberating from the Japanese Occupation, (1945) the Korean government has invested much time and effort into rebuilding, restoring, and reversing the damages done during the Japanese Occupation,

창덕궁 Chang Deok Gung

Changdeokgung Palace ("Prospering Virtue Palace"), just like Changgyeonggung Palce, is also known as Donggwol, ("Eastern Palace"), because of its location which sits to the east of Gyeongbokgung Palace. This beautiful palace was home to the Joseon government, as well as a beloved residence of numerous kings of the Joseon Dynasty, and for this reason, it was the longest-serving royal residential palace. Its unique beauty comes from the fact that it flawlessly blends into its surrounding nature and landscape, and Huwon, the palace's rear garden, and the only rear garden of any Korean palace, is the essence of Korean landscaping, and it occupies about sixty percent of the palace! The garden design contains Joseon's philosophy of art. Luckily, Changdeokgung Palace is well-preserved compared to other palaces that were damaged and destroyed throughout history, and many of its original features still remain intact. As such, it was added to the UNESCO World Heritage List in 1997.

덕수궁 Deok Su Gung

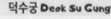

Deoksugung Palace is different from other Korean palaces as it contains a harmonious mixture of medieval and modern style architecture. For example - you will find a modern seal engraved a western-style garden and fountain. Originally, Deoksugung was not a palace. When the fourteenth king of the Joseon Dynasty, King Seonjo, returedn from his evacuation caused by the Imjin War (Japanese invasions in 1592), all palaces were severely damaged. For that reason, Deoksugung was chosen as a temporary residence for the royal family. The fifteenth king, King Gwanghaegun, renamed it to Gyeonggunung, and formalized it as a royal palace, and Emperor Gojong of the Korean Empire (also the twenty-sixth king of the Joseon Dynasty), stayed here and expanded it. During the Joseon Dynasty, the royal guard was responsible for opening and closing the palace gate as well as patrolling, and you can see the reenactment taking place today when you visit. Another very popular spot is the stone wall surrounding the palace, although there is an urban legend that says couples will break up if they walk down along the wall!

충무공 이순신 Chung Mu Gong Yi Sun-sin

Yi Sun-sin 이순신 (1545 – 1598) was a Korean naval commander/admiral, and is arguably the most beloved and revered figure in the entire Korean history. Famed for his incredible victories against the Japanese navy during the Imjin War (Japanese invasions) during the Joseon Dynasty era, as well as his exemplary moral conduct on and off the battlefield. For this reason, he was not only respected by Koreans, but by Japanese admirals as well. Military historians praised Admiral Yi Sun-Sin as one of the greatest naval commanders in history, on par with Admiral Horatio Nelson for his undefeated record against seemingly insurmountable odds. His title of Samdo Sugun Tongjesa 삼도수군통제사 ("Naval Commander of the Three Provinces") was the title for the commander of the Korean navy until 1896. His most remarkable military achievement, which has been made into a movie as well, occurred at the Battle of Myeongnyang, where the Joseon navy was outnumbered by 133 warships to 13, and forced into a last stand. But with only his minimal fleet standing between the Japanese Army and the capital Hanyang, he led the navy to repel the Japanese force, leaving 31 of the 133 enemy warships either destroyed or impaired, without losing a single ship of his own. One of his greatest accomplishments was resurrecting and improving the turtle ship, or geobukseon (거북선), whose original design was suggested during the reign of King Taejong. Using his creative mind and with the support of his subordinates, the armored ship was brought back to life and played an important role in defeating the Japanese. He died at the Battle of Noryang on December 16, 1598. On the verge of completely expelling the Japanese force from the Korean Peninsula, he was mortally wounded by an enemy bullet. Even during his last moments of life, he left the following last words "The battle is at its height...beat my war drums...do not announce my death." After death, the royal court bestowed various honors upon him, including a posthumous title of Chungmugong (충무공; Duke of Loyalty and Warfare), a recognition as a Seonmu Ildeung Gongsin (선무일등공신;First-class military order of merit), and two posthumous offices, Yeonguijeong (영의정; Prime Minister), and the Deokpung Buwongun (덕풍부원군; The Prince of the Court from Deokpung). Admiral Yi Sun-sin remains a venerated hero among Koreans, and you can find his face and the turtle ship on the 100 Korean Won and 5 Korean Won coins today.

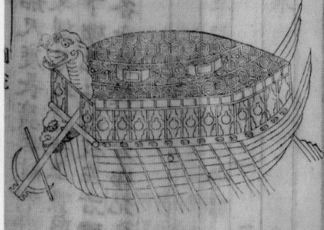

16th century Korean turtle ship in a depiction dating to 1795. The woodblock print is based on a contemporary, late 18th century model.
PHGCOM [CC BY-SA 3.0 (http://creativecommons.org/licenses/by-sa/3.0/)]

Dreaming of a Modern State, The Korean Empire (1897 ˜ 1910)

1897   **Proclamation of the Empire** - **King Gojong** returns after 1 year of refugee at the Russian Legation.

1905   **Korea-Japan Treaty of 1905** gives Japan complete power for Korea's foreign affairs and placed all trade through Korean ports under Japanese supervision.

1907   June - **The Hague Secret Emissary Affair**

July - **Emperor Gojong abdicated** by the Japanese Imperialists, and Gojong's son **Sunjong** succeeded to the throne.

1909   **Ito Hirobumi** (Japanese Resident-General of Korea) **assassinated** by Korean general and independence activist **An Jung-geun**.

1910   **The Japan-Korea Treaty of 1910** started the annexation of the Korean Empire by Imperial Japan.

고종 황제 Emperor Go Jong

Gojong, the Gwangmu Emperor (1852 – 1919), was the twenty-sixth and final king of the Joseon Dynasty. During his reign, he was influenced by Empress Myeong Seong (Queen Min), and unlike his father Heungseon Daewongun, who maintained a closed-door/national-isolation policy, he adopted an open-door foreign policy. For example, he signed a Treaty of Amity and Trade with the US in 1882, although it was done in hopes of gaining protection from Imperial Japan, China, and Russia. While the conflict among three neighboring powerhouses was rising, Gojong proclaimed Korea an empire in 1897, and he became the first Emperor, Gwangmu, and the Joseon Dynasty ended at the same time. In an effort to maintain Korean sovereignty, he played and leveraged on the power struggle and rivalry among the rivals, effectively preventing each of them from having total control over Korea. His efforts finally came to an end after the Russo-Japanese War (1904–05).

을사조약 Eulsa Treaty

Victorious Japan forced Gojong to accept pro-Japanese advisors to the royal court, which in turn, led him to sign the Protectorate Treaty of 1905 (also known as "Eulsa Treaty") between Korea and Japan. As a result, Korea lost its status and rights as an independent sovereign nation.

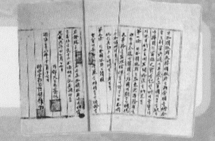

The Hague Secret Emissary Affair

Gojong secretly sent representatives (Yi Tjoune 이준, Yi Sang-seol 이상설 and Yi Wi-jong 이위종, more commonly known today as "Hague Secret Emissary Affair", to the Hague Peace Convention in 1907, to assert the Korean sovereignty, and to declare the invalidity of Japanese diplomatic maneuvers, including the Japan–Korea Treaty of 1905. At the convention, the representatives asserted the monarch's rights to rule Korea independent of Japan. Sadly, the emissaries were not allowed by the nations to take part in the conference. Eventually, though, they managed to hold interviews with newspapers and spoke out about the unfairness being done by the Japanese. As a result, the enraged Japanese forced Gojong to abdicate, and his son Sunjong was put to the throne, and ruled for just three years before the Korean Empire ended with the annexation of Korea by Japan in 1910. Just like that the empire dissolved, and was never re-established.

Sad History – Japanese Colonial Period (1910 ~ 1945)

1916 The final wave of **Uibyeong** rebels is defeated by Japanese forces.

1919 Spurred by the sudden and mysterious death of Gojong, **March 1st Movement**, organized by **Yu Gwan Sun** began. **Declaration of Korean Independence. Nationwide peaceful demonstrations** are crushed by Japanese military and police forces after two months. **Governor-General Hasegawa** resigns.

The establishment of **The Provisional Government of the Republic of Korea in Shanghai.**

1920 **Battle of Cheongsanri**, Korean independence Army, led by **Kim Jwa-jin**, victory.

1932 Korean independence activist **Lee Bong Chang** fails in his attempt to assassinate Emperor Hirohito in Tokyo.

Korean independence activist **Yun Bong Gil** bombs Japanese Military gathering in Shanghai.

1945 **The Empire of Japan surrenders** to the Allies. According to the terms of Potsdam Declaration, **Korea becomes independent.**

안중근 Ahn Jung Geun

Ahn Jung-geun, 안중근 (1879 – 1910) was a Korean-independence activist, who assassinated Prince Itō Hirobumi, a four-time Prime Minister of Japan, former Resident-General of Korea, and then President of the Privy Council of Japan in 1909, immediately after the signing of the Eulsa Treaty, which put Korea on the verge of annexation by Japan. In October 1909,. Itō had come back to Harbin Railway Station from negotiating with the Russian representative on the train. Passing the imperial Japanese guards, Ahn shot Itō three times on the railway platform, and yelled out the slogan for Korean independence in Russian, waving the Korean flag. After getting captured by the Russian guards, Ahn insisted that he be treated as a prisoner of war, as a lieutenant general of the Korean resistance army, instead of a criminal, but was hanged as a common criminal. Ahn was posthumously awarded the Order of Merit for National Foundation in 1962 by the South Korean government, the most prestigious civil decoration in the Republic of Korea, in recognition for his efforts towards Korean independence.

March 1st Movement & 유관순 Yu Gwan Sun

Yu Gwan-sun 유관순 (1902 – 1920) is a symbol of Korea's fight for independence against imperial Japan, and an organizer of the March 1st Movement, one of the earliest public displays of Korean resistance during the period of Japanese occupation (1910 ~ 1919). The name literally means "Three-One Movement" or "March First Movement" in Korean, as it took place on March 1st, 1919. It was a peaceful protest where thousands of Koreans gathered to cry out "Long Live Korean Independence! (Korean: dae han dok lip man se! 대한독립만세!), while waving the Korean flag in the air. Yu, along with other activists, planned a large scale protest which took place in Aunae Marketplace at 9:00 a.m. Approximately 3,000 demonstrators rallied, and it went on for hours, until the Japanese military police arrived and fired on the unarmed Korean protesters, killing 19, including Yu's parents. Yu was arrested, and was severely tortured and interrogated, but refused to give information on the identity or whereabouts of her collaborators. Yu later died in jail from the aftereffects of torture.

KOREAN WAR
TIMELINE

Aug 15 1945

Free At Last
Japan surrenders following the WWII defeat. As a result, the Japanese occupation ended and Korea was liberated.

The Division
Fundamental shifts in global politics and ideology led to the division of Korea into two occupation zones - the US administering the southern half and the Soviet Union the northern half of the 38th parallel.

 VS

Dr. Syngman Rhee (1875-1965)
First President of South Korea

Kim IL-SUNG (1948-1994)
First Supreme Leader of North Korea

North Invades South
At the dawn of June 25, 1950, North Korean forces began the sudden invasion of South Korea, triggering the Korean War

Jun 25 1950

Jun 27 1950

US Joins The War
President Harry Truman deploys troops, hoping to stop the spread of Communism to South Korea.

Sep 15 1950

Victory At Incheon
Commanded by General MacArthur, the UN forces successfully executes an amphibious invasion which resulted in a decisive victory and strategic reversal.

China Joins The War
The Communist China, which bordered North Korea, started worrying about protecting themsleves, and sent a massive amount of troops, making important victories that pushed the UN troops back acorss the 38th parallel.

Oct 1950

Feb 1 1951

Peace Talks Begin
With the battling at a stalemate, peace talks began, but it will take two years for the opposite sides to reach an agreement.

Jun 27 1953

Truce Reached
Armistice agreement ends a 3-year-long brutal war between two Koreas.

Talks Fail To Unite
US and Chinese representatives meet to discuss the terms but fail to reach an agreement, leaving Korea divided.

Apr 1954

Post Korean War (1953 ~ Today)

1960   **April Revolution** overthrows the autocratic **Rhee administration.** Rhee resigns and goes into exile. **Yun Bo Seon** becomes the President.

1961   **General Park Chung Hee**, overthrows the government through a military coup and becomes President.

1962   Start of the **Five-year plans** of South Korea.

1964   South Korea joins **Vietnam War.**

1970   Start of the government-operated **New Community Movement.**

1976   **The Axe Murder Incident in Panmunjom**, Joint Security Area. Triggers former North Korean leader Kim il-sung's first official apology to the South.

1977   South Korea celebrates **10 billion dollars gained by exports**.

1979   President **Park Chung Hee** is **assassinated** by chief of KCIA, **Kim Jaegyu.**

1980   **General Chun Doo Hwan** gets military power through a coup and becomes the President.

        Gwangju Uprising. Martial Law is declared throughout the nation.

1987   **June Democracy Movement** overthrows the autocratic Chun regime. The ruling party of Fifth Republic, Democratic Justice Party, declares democratic elections.

1988   24th **Summer Olympic Games** held in **Seoul.**

1991   **North Korea** and **South Korea** join the **United Nations (UN).**

1992   **South Korea's first satellite**, KITSAT-1, a.k.a. **Uri Byol** is **successfully launched.**

1993   **Test of Rodong-1**, a single stage, mobile liquid propellant medium range ballistic missile by North Korea.

1994   **Kim Jong Il** takes control of North Korea upon the death of his father **Kim Il-Sung**. Start of the **Arduous March**.

1999   **North Korea** promises to **freeze long-range missile** tests.

2000   The **first summit** between North Korean leader **Kim Jong Il** and South Korean President **Kim Dae Jung** is held.

2002   The 2002 **FIFA World Cup jointly held by Korea & Japan**. North Korea pledges to extend **moratorium on missile tests** beyond 2003.

2006   Test of **Taepodong-2 missile**. There is a **nuclear test** in North Korea. US officials assert it might have been a misfire.

2007   **The second summit** is held, with **Roh Moo-hyun** (South) and **Kim Jong Il** (North) representing each side. North Korea fires **short-range missile** into the East Sea.

2010   **North Korea** launches missile and **attacks Korean Pohang class corvette, ROKS Cheonan.**

        In November, North Korean army rains **artillery fire** on Yeon-Pyeong-Do island.

2011   **Kim Jong Il dies**, **Kim Jong un** takes over as the **Supreme Leader of North Korea.**

April Revolution

The April Revolution, was a large scale uprising led by labor and student groups, triggered by the discovery in Masan Harbor of the body of a high school student Kim Ju-yul, killed by a tear-gas shell during his participation in demonstrations against a fixed election by then ruling party of Korea in March 1960. As a result, a series of protests led to the eventual resignation of the Rhee administration and the transition to the Second Republic of South Korea.

Rhee Syngman

Syngman Rhee 이승만 (March 26, 1875 – July 19, 1965), was the first president of South Korea. During his early years, he was educated in the U.S., at George Washington University, Harvard, and Princeton University, and part of this reason is because of his nationalist activities against the Japanese occupation of Korea which forced him to live in exile in Hawaii and Shanghai. He originally served (1920 - 1925) as president of the Korean Provisional Government in Shanghai, until he was expelled by Kim Ku. From 1934 until 1944, he zealously campaigned in New York and Washington D.C., trying to win international support for Korean independence. After World War II, General MacArthur ordered his return to South Korea. Capitalizing on his closeness and familiarity with the United States, Rhee effectively campaigned for the immediate independence and unification of Korea and soon built up a mass political organization. As a result, Rhee was able to be elected the first president of South Korea in 1948. He was re-elected for three consecutive terms. His presidency, which covered 1948 to April 1960, remains controversial among historians today because of his authoritarian government, but is highly regarded due to his achievements as a strong anti-Communist, and a leader who led South Korea through the Korean War. His presidency ended in resignation following the April Revolution. He died in exile in Hawaii.

Kim Il Sung

Kim Il-sung 김일성(April 1912 – 8 July 1994) was the first leader of North Korea which he ruled from the country's establishment in 1948 until his death in 1994. Coming to power after the end of Japanese rule in 1945, backed by the Soviet support, he authorized the illegal invasion of South Korea in 1950, triggering an intervention in defense of South Korea by the United Nations led by the United States, which eventually led to the full-blown Korean War (1950 ~ 1953). Under his leadership, North Korea became a communist state, with close political and economic ties with the Soviet Union. By the 1960s, North Korea reached a standard of living higher than the South, which was struggling with political instability that also hindered the economic growth. The situation reversed in the mid-1970s, however, as a newly stable South Korea under the leadership of president Park Chung Hee became an economic powerhouse fueled by U.S. and Japanese investment. Economic development in North Korea stagnated, and it exacerbated when the support from the Soviet Union ended in 1991, with the dissolution of the USSR. And the gap has been continuously widening until today. During Kim Il Sung's rule, North Korea was a totalitarian state with serious human rights abuses, including mass executions and prison camps.

Park Chung Hee

Park Chung Hee 박정희 (November 1917 – 26 October 1979) was a South Korean politician and general who served as the President of South Korea from 1963 to 1979. Park assumed the office after initially ruling the nation as head of a military dictatorship installed by the coup he led in 1961. Before he too over the control and became president, he was a military leader in the South Korean army and served as the chairman of the Supreme Council for National Reconstruction (1961 – 1963). Park's successful coup ended the interim government (Second Republic) and started the Third Republic. During his reign, he declared martial law and amended the constitution into a highly authoritarian form, termed the Yushin Constitution. Park had led a series of monumental campaigns that transformed devastated nation into an economic powerhouse, which is better known today as the "Miracle of The Han River". Despite this, there was a political discourse among the people in the office, and Park was assassinated by his close friend Kim Jae-gyu, the then director of the KCIA (Korean central Intelligence Agency). After death, South Korea's economic growth continued thanks to the strong foundations established under Park's leadership. Although some criticize the fact that such economic growth was achieved at the expense of civil liberties, he's considered and revered as one of the most greatest South Korean presidents who reshaped and modernized the nation.

For your Korean study needs,
check out our other titles!
at newampersand.com

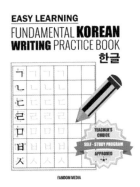

Let's Study Korean - Complete Practice Work Book for Grammar, Spelling, Vocabulary and Reading Comprehension With Over 600 Questions
Let's Speak Korean- Learn Over 1,400 Expressions Quickly and Easily With Pronunciation & Grammar Guide Marks - Just Listen, Repeat, & Learn!
Fun & Easy Korean-English Picture Dictionary - Fastest Way To Learn Over 1,000+ Words and Expressions
Quick & Easy Korean Vocabulary - 1,000 Essential Words and Phrases with Pronunciation Guide
Easy Learning Fundamental Korean Writing Practice Book

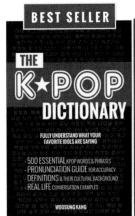
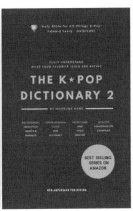
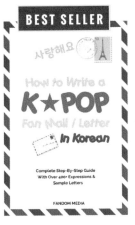

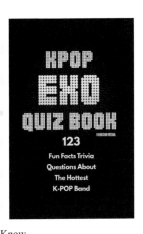

The K-Pop Dictionary - 500 Essential Korean Slang Words and Phrases Every K-Pop, K-Drama, K-Movie Fan Should Know
The K-Pop Dictionary 2 - Learn To Understand What Your Favorite Korean Idols Are Saying On M/V, Drama, and TV Shows
How To Write a K-Pop Fan Mail / Letter in Korean - Complete Step-By-Step Guide With Over 400+ Expressions & Sample Letters
K-Pop BTS Quiz Book - 123 Fun Facts Trivia Questions About K-Pop's Hottest Band
K-Pop EXO Quiz Book - 123 Fun Facts Trivia Questions About K-Pop's Hottest Band

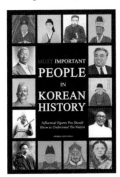

Most Important People in Korean Histor
Influential Figures You Should Know To Understand The Nation

Best Korean Short Stories Collection 1 ~ 3 (Korean Edition)
Meet the Essence of Korean Literature

Admiral Yi Sun-Sin (Soon-Shin) (Korean Edition)
The Legendary Turtle Ship War Hero

KOREA AT A GLANCE :
Quick and Easy Visual Book To Help You Learn and Understand Korea !
ISBN 9791188195503

Copyright © 2019 by Fandom Media

Ordering Information: Quantity sales. Special discounts are available on quantity purchases by corporations, associations, and others. For details, contact the publisher at the email address above.

Printed in the United States of America

www.newampersand.com

14 13 12 11 10 / 10 9 8 7 6 5 4 3 2 1

Printed in Great Britain
by Amazon